People from the Past

WELDON OWEN PTY LTD

Chairman: John Owen
Publisher: Sheena Coupe
Associate Publisher: Lynn Humphries
Managing Editor: Helen Bateman
Design Concept: Sue Rawkins
Senior Designer: Kylie Mulquin
Production Manager: Caroline Webber
Production Assistant: Kylie Lawson

Text: Robert Coupe
Consultant: Colin Sale, Geography Lecturer and Author

04 03 02 01 00 99
10 9 8 7 6 5 4 3 2 1

Published in New Zealand by Shortland Publications,
2B Cawley Street, Ellerslie, Auckland.
Published in the United Kingdom by Kingscourt Publishing Limited,
P.O. Box 1427, Freepost, London W6 9BR.
Published in Australia by Shortland–Mimosa,
8 Yarra Street, Hawthorn, Victoria 3122.

Printed in Australia.
ISBN: 0-7699-0534-X

CONTENTS

China   4

Egypt   10

Greece   16

Rome   22

The Americas   28

Glossary   30

Index   31

A RICH WOMAN

This woman's long silk skirt and jacket and the gold ornaments in her hair show that she came from a well-to-do family.

MEN'S FASHION

This is how a rich young man would have looked in China more than 1,000 years ago. Clothes in ancient China were coloured with vegetable dyes.

FAMILY RULES

Children in ancient China were taught to obey their parents strictly. A wife, too, had to obey her husband and her husband's parents.

CHINA

China is one of the world's oldest civilizations. The people of modern China can trace their origins back to ancestors who lived in China more than 8,000 years ago. Family life was very important in ancient Chinese society, as it still is today. Grandparents, uncles, aunts, parents and children often lived together in the same house. Wealthy Chinese people dressed in richly coloured clothes made of embroidered silks.

Most people in ancient China belonged to a particular group or class. Peasants grew food and raised animals. Artisans, such as carpenters and potters, were skilled at making things with their hands. Merchants were business people who bought and sold goods, and sometimes became extremely wealthy. Scholars were the most respected people in Chinese society. They were often the only ones who could read and write. The magistrate in the red robes, opposite, would have belonged to the scholar class.

scholar

peasant

artisan

merchant

Did You Know?

The Chinese had machines that drew water for crops from canals and rivers in times of drought. Peasants had to pedal the machines to pump up the water.

AT COURT

Chinese emperors and their families and advisers wore fine silk and lived in rich palaces. Visitors to the court brought elaborate gifts to win the emperor's favour.

TOMBS

Many Chinese believed in a life after death. They decorated the tombs of rich and important people with paintings, and left wine and food for the person who had died.

The most powerful person in ancient China was the emperor. The people called their emperors "Sons of Heaven". They believed that an emperor ruled with the approval of former emperors who had died and were now in heaven. Rulers also believed that these earlier emperors could help them to rule wisely and could protect them and their subjects from accidents and misfortune. When tragedies such as earthquakes, floods or famines occurred, people often thought that the heavenly spirits were punishing their emperor for being a weak, lazy or selfish leader.

MAKE A CARTOUCHE

Step one

Step two

Step three

Step four

What you need
- 1½ cups of flour
- 1 cup of salt
- ½ cup of water
- paints
- bowl
- rolling pin
- knife
- baking tray
- stick
- oven

An ancient Egyptian cartouche was a sign with hieroglyphs on it.

1 Mix the flour and salt and stir in the water.

2 Knead the mixture into a dough and roll it out with a rolling pin.

3 Cut it into an oval shape, carve your own hieroglyphs in it with a stick, and bake it till it is dry.

4 Paint your cartouche with different colours.

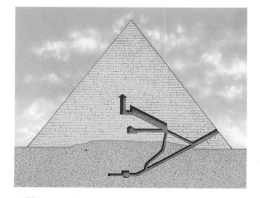

ROOMS AND PASSAGEWAYS
Passages and chambers were built deep inside a pharaoh's pyramid.

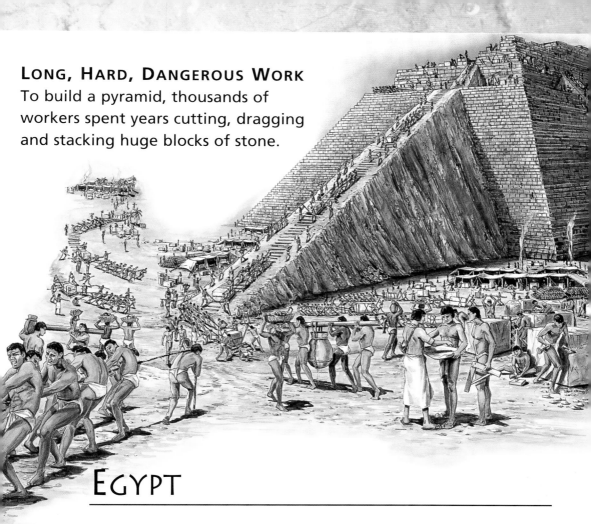

LONG, HARD, DANGEROUS WORK

To build a pyramid, thousands of workers spent years cutting, dragging and stacking huge blocks of stone.

EGYPT

Almost 5,000 years ago, Egypt became a powerful nation in the ancient world. For more than 2,000 years, leaders called pharaohs ruled this country. Pharaohs built enormous tombs or pyramids that were as big as palaces, and filled them with precious objects. They believed they would take these things with them to another life after they died.

11

The ancient Egyptians lived beside the great Nile River. They depended on its water for drinking, for washing and for growing crops. The river was their main means of transport. It was also the home of fish, water fowl and other animals, such as the hippopotamus, that the Egyptians hunted and ate. Along the banks of the Nile grew a reed called papyrus. The Egyptians used it to make boats, fishing nets, paper and many other things.

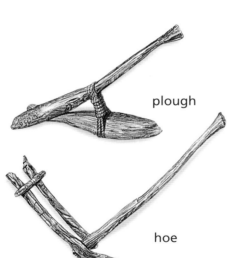

plough

hoe

FARMING TOOLS
Egyptians were expert farmers. They had hoes for loosening the earth and ploughs for turning it over.

papyrus reeds

DID YOU KNOW?

About 5,000 years ago the Egyptians found a way of making a kind of paper out of papyrus reeds. They also wove it into baskets, boxes and even sandals.

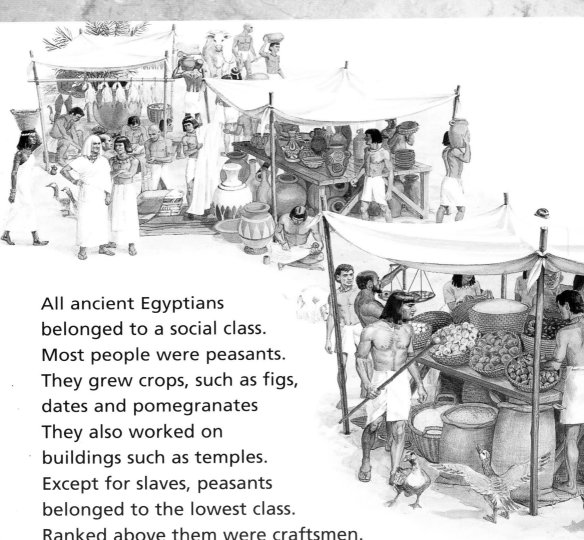

All ancient Egyptians
belonged to a social class.
Most people were peasants.
They grew crops, such as figs,
dates and pomegranates
They also worked on
buildings such as temples.
Except for slaves, peasants
belonged to the lowest class.
Ranked above them were craftsmen.
Higher up were scribes. Because they could
write, scribes often had a lot of power. In the highest class
of all were people who ran the government and temples or
who were in charge of different regions of Egypt. Many of
these were members of the pharaoh's family.

LIFE AT THE PHARAOH'S COURT

A pharaoh was treated as if he were a god. People believed he could control things like the weather and how crops grew.

WOMEN AT WORK

Women were able to own property, but they did not have positions of power. They often did jobs such as grinding grain, baking bread and spinning flax.

GREECE

About 2,500 years ago, Greece became a very important country in the ancient world, and its influence is still felt today. Much of our mathematics, architecture and art

developed from the knowledge of the ancient Greeks. The first Olympic Games were held in ancient Greece. In addition to studying numerous writings, archaeologists have learned a lot about the Greeks from jugs and other containers that potters made and decorated.

OPEN-AIR THEATRE

Greek men and women went to large outdoor theatres to see their favourite plays. Many of these plays are still performed today.

DID YOU KNOW?

Dinner parties in ancient Greece were called symposiums. Only men attended them— women were not allowed, except as performers.

Schools in ancient Greece were run by private teachers. If their parents could afford it, Greek boys were sent to school when they were about six. They learned to read and write, and to do mathematics. Writing exercises were done on special wooden tablets covered with soft wax. The boys wrote into the wax with a sharp instrument called a stylus. A slave owned by the family would go with the boys and punish them if they did not pay attention. Girls were not sent to school, but some learned reading and writing at home.

GREEK LETTERS

The Greeks used 24 letters to spell out their words. The first two were "alpha" and "beta". That's where the English word "alphabet" comes from.

AMAZING!

Pan was a mythical Greek spirit, half man and half goat. He played a set of pipes made from reeds.

MUSIC LESSONS

Boys went to a special teacher to learn to play instruments such as the lyre the boy is being handed above. The same teacher also taught them poetry.

19

Democracy began in Greece. In a democracy, citizens vote to choose their leaders. In ancient Athens, only men could become citizens. Any citizen could speak at a big public meeting, called an assembly. When the speakers had finished, everyone voted on whether to pass or change the laws discussed. Trial by jury also came to us from the Greeks. When someone was accused of a crime, juries of more than 200 citizens would decide whether the person was innocent or guilty.

TIME RUNNING OUT

At a trial, any citizen could speak for or against an accused person. Each citizen had to stop speaking when all the water from one pot had dripped into another pot placed below.

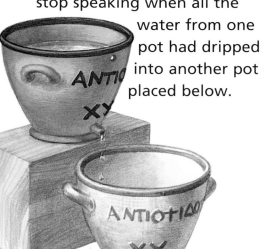

THE JURY'S VERDICT

Each jury member had two brass tokens, one with a hollow centre and one with a solid centre. At the end of the trial, the jury voted with these tokens—hollow for innocent, solid for guilty.

DID YOU KNOW?

Slaves were bought and sold in Greek markets. They did most of the housework for rich families. Slaves in Greece were often trusted and well treated.

ROME

The Romans ruled over large areas of Europe for hundreds of years, until about 1,500 years ago. They also controlled most of the countries around the Mediterranean Sea. Many of the buildings that the Romans constructed are still standing. Some of the largest are temples, built to honour the Roman gods and goddesses. Some temples were built to Jupiter, the ruler of all the gods. Some were built to Mars, the god of war, or to Venus, the goddess of love. People also worshipped the emperors of Rome as gods and built temples in their honour.

SERVANTS OF VESTA
Vesta was the goddess of the hearth, or home. Her shrine in Rome had a flame that was always kept burning. Six women known as the Vestal Virgins were chosen to look after this shrine.

A TEMPLE TO ALL THE GODS

The Pantheon was built almost 2,000 years
ago. It contained a separate altar for each of
the Roman gods. Tourists who go to Rome
can still visit this great building.

A ROMAN WEDDING

At her wedding, a young Roman woman
wore an orange veil and a garland of
marjoram on her head. Sometimes a young
woman did not choose her own husband,
but married a man chosen by her father.

Women and girls wore simple dresses or long, flowing robes. Men wore garments called togas—long pieces of material wrapped loosely around the body. Wealthy men, like the one shown below, wore togas with purple around their edges.

LIFE AT HOME
The father was the head of the family. Here the mother holds a charm to protect the baby.

25

SIEGE

This fort stands high on a rock at Masada, in Israel. About 2,000 years ago, Roman troops captured it, using a huge tower, shown left, to climb up the wall.

Roman armies were highly organized. They were divided into legions of about 5,000 soldiers. A centurion, like the officer with the crest on the left in the illustration, was in charge of a hundred men. Legions of Roman soldiers marched off to battle, or to conquer new lands. Soldiers were well trained and very disciplined. Many poor young men joined the army for the small amount of pay they received. They had to serve for 25 years before they could retire.

STRANGE BUT TRUE

Groups of Roman soldiers sometimes protected themselves from arrows and other weapons by holding their shields around and above them as they moved into battle.

DEADLY WEAPON

Romans used catapults to fire large stones. These stones could break through the walls of forts like the one at Masada.

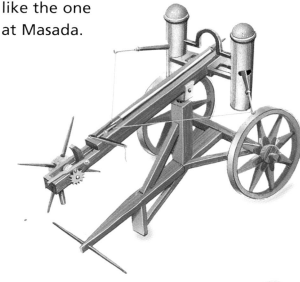

THE AMERICAS

Until about 500 years ago, most people of the Americas had not seen or heard of European people. During the 16th century, soldiers from Spain conquered many of the lands they lived in. The lives of peoples such as the Aztecs and the Maya in Mexico and the Inca in Peru were badly disrupted. Much of their civilization, which had built up over many centuries, was destroyed.

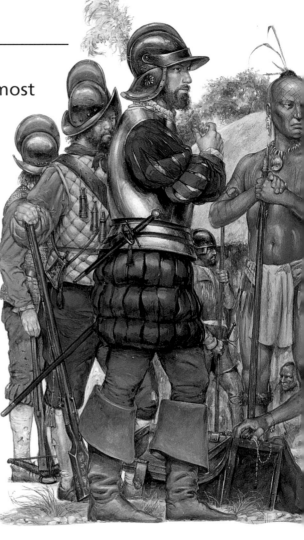

ANCIENT JEWELLERY
This ornament was made by Aztec craftspeople many centuries ago.

ANCIENT CITY

Mayan people built this pyramid, found in the Great Plaza, in their city of Tikal. At the top of its giant stairway is a temple that only priests were allowed to enter.

STORIES IN STONE

The Maya used carved stones called "stelae" to record the dates and the main events of their rulers' lives. Some stelae had pictures of the rulers carved on them.

GLOSSARY

archaeologist A person who studies the remains of past human lives and activities.

Aztec The name of the people who settled in Mexico about 800 years ago.

Incas The name of the people who settled in Peru about 900 years ago.

magistrate A person in charge of the trial of someone accused of an offence.

Maya Ancient peoples who built up a great civilization in parts of North America and Central America. The Mayan civilization reached the height of its power more than 1,000 years ago.

pharaohs The name of the rulers of ancient Egypt.

pyramid A pointed, shaped building with sides in the shape of triangles.

scribes Powerful people in ancient Egypt who could read and write. They kept records of trade and business and carved signs on temples, tombs and other buildings.

shrine A special place where a Roman or Greek god or goddess was honoured.

INDEX

alphabet	18
beliefs	9, 11, 15
cartouches	10
catapults	27
class structure	6, 14, 15
clothing	4–5, 8, 24, 25
democracy	20
emperors	8–9, 22
family life	4–5, 24–25
farming	6, 7, 12, 14, 15
juries	20
papyrus	12, 13
pharaohs	10, 11, 14, 15
pyramids	10–11
schooling	18–19
slaves	14, 18, 21
soldiers	26–27, 28
temples	14, 22, 23, 29

CREDITS AND NOTES

PICTURE AND ILLUSTRATION CREDITS
[t=top, b=bottom, l=left, r=right, c=centre, F=front, B=back, C=cover, bg=background]
Susanna Addario 29tr. **Paul Bachem** 8–9cl, 12–13c, 13rc, 13tr, BC. **Kenn Backhaus** 3br, 22bl. **Jim Chan** 10tl. **Corel Corporation** 29bc. **Mike Gorman** 10bl. **Ray Grinaway** 26–27bc. **Adam Hook/Bernard Thornton Artists UK** 17cl. **Christa Hook/Bernard Thornton Artists UK** 17br, 18–19c, 18–19bc, FCtl. **Richard Hook/Bernard Thornton Artists UK** 15tr, 28–29c. **Janet Jones** 1c, 2bl, 4–5br, 6br, 6bc, 6c, 6cl, 7tc, 14–15lc, 15br, 16bc, 20bl, 20cr, 21tc, 25bc, FCbc. **Shane Marsh/Linden Artists Ltd** 7br. **Peter Mennim** 4bl, 4c, 24tc, 31br. **Steve Noon/illustration** 21bc. **Darren Pattenden/illustration** 9tr. **PhotoEssentials** 4–32 borders, Cbg. **Evert Ploeg** 10–11rc. **John Richards** 26tl. **Michael Saunders** 28bl, FCtr. **C. Winston Taylor** 12lc. **Steve Trevaskis** 19tl. **Rod Westblade** 27tr, 27br, 30tc. **Ann Winterbotham** 23c.

ACKNOWLEDGEMENTS
Weldon Owen would like to thank the following people for their assistance in the production of this book: Jocelyne Best, Peta Gorman, Tracey Jackson, Andrew Kelly, Sarah Mattern, Emily Wood.